Go to the Living

Go to the Living
Copyright 2017 by Micah Chatterton
ISBN: 978-0-9970932-6-1
All rights reserved

No part of this book may be used or reproduced in any manner whatsoever without the prior written permission of both the publisher and the copyright owner.

Cover art: "Ezra's Names" by Micah Chatterton
Book design and layout by Lawrence Eby

Printed and bound in the United States
Distributed by Ingram

Published by Inlandia Institute
Riverside, California
www.inlandiainstitute.org
First Edition

Go to the Living

Micah Chatterton

Contents

First, Language	11
—Toward Tulum, November	14
Metaphor Game	15
—Nohoch Mul	16
Zoo Tanka	17
—Big Sur	19
Undated Photograph (PICU)	21
—Pascagoula	23
First Dream after Seizing	24
—Forest Falls	26
Dear Dad, Father, Sensei, Royal Kicker of Asses	27
Now, Someday	28
—Coronado	30
I Can Take It	31
What I Said	33
—Riverside	35
Condolences	36
—Kitchen Counter	38
First Dream of Becoming Ash	39
—Liquidambar	43
Questions	45
Self-Hypnosis	51
South Wichita Safeway	59
—Pomegranate Tree, June	60
Young Couple	61
—Na'Pali	62
Flagstaff	63
—Secret Falls	64
Snabu	65
—Nu'uanu Pali	66
Armadillo	67
—Byodo-In Temple	68
Grandpa	69
—Manoa	70
Custer's Last Haircut	71

—Keyhole	73
Negligent Avocadicide	74
—Library, July 20th	76
Lucky	77
—Hillside	79
Folk Medicine	80
—Reveille	82
First Dream of Kinship	83
—Los Angeles	84
Love to All, S~	85
—Ultrasound	87
A Love Poem	88
—North Ponto	89
Sand	90
—Fig Grove, July 20th	91
A Story I Remembered this Morning...	92
—Labor & Delivery	94
First Dream in Which the Wind Speaks for...	95
—North Ponto and a Year	96
Notes from the Life After	97
—Children's Hospital	99
Bedtime Tanka	100
—Evergreen Memorial Park & Mausoleum	101
Sphinx	102
—Horse Run, October 20th	106
Dropped Tanka	107
—Gaviota	109
Easter Morning	110
—Henry Cowell Redwoods	112
Undated Photograph (Beach)	113
—Roberts Ranch, Behind the Preschool, October 20th	115
Bread	116
A Note on Forms	121
Notes on Places	122
Acknowledgements	127

For Ezra, who made me—

—For Samuel, who saved me

First, Language

1

La lengua, tongue.
La sal, salt.

He's old enough now to know:
naming a thing needs touch, means
he has to wade in to his shins and grasp
for it with his whole arm cold and dripping.
Quartz, jasper, driftwood: he's been fishing
pebbles from the creek for an hour, to hold
in the thin lever of his hand and call out to me
before he slings. He scours the shallows
for unlike specimens, fascinated
by the licked smoothness, the heft, plunk
and slither of a stone disappearing in water.
He snags a bit of pitted limestone from the sand,
smelting ore for the forty foot limekilns
in the forest at creek's head, ferns spilling
from every rust-break. *This one?* he asks.
Distracted, I tease my embers with a split branch.
This one? he presses, cradling the question to my face.

I sniff the damp stone in the cave of his hand,
the earth of it, and pause. *It's a marshmallow.*
Coals crackle with his laugh.
Take a bite, I say. *Daddies can't lie.*

2

We read 'Song of the Redwood-Tree'
in our sleeping bags. His breathing
begins to match the cadence of my voice

as he drifts off. I can't tell what he hears,
what words he recognizes— *song axes
soul forest falling*— needles, heartwood,
bark enough to build into a tree.
Or not. How many words wash through him,
scales fanning in a current, each with a picture,
gone in a second? How many bank themselves
into the walls of his body?

3

He kicks in his sleep, running in place.
He rolls, his socked feet pulling the lip
of the blanket past his belly button.
What do I tell him when he wakes?
Do I hunker up beside him, listlessly
fishing onions out of his scrambled eggs?
Do I lay my hand on his back?
If, when my mouth fills up with clay,
do I draw us out in the dirt, the shape
of our family now?

> See, son,
> here are the two houses,
> each its own box and triangle,
> and two sexless stick people
> standing at each house, and here,
> a smaller figure, white plate
> for a head, arms pulled straight,
> floating between them.

Do I make him say it?

4

We teeter, stack ourselves in the surf.
He scissors my neck with his thighs
and grips my hair like a pony's. When the water
rises, I dip his heels in. A shriek and a laugh,

he loves and hates the cold ocean at once.
A fish darts by a few feet away, glinting like a coin
of light, like the reflection off a wristwatch,
and swims through my legs, our legs.

5

The green-slicked creek pours over the lip
of the cliff, adding its body to the ocean's,
fresh thread leaping into a mass of blue cloth.
In the space between waves, the inlet becomes
silent, drops foaming on the rockline before
a huge tongue of water jams back, cracking
the walls with its enormity. He times his throws
to these silences so he can hear the splash
of the rock. He is fearless, my son, amazed
by the cliff-splitting sea, the salt smell, the pampas
tapping his back, the fog slipping around the necks
of redwoods in the distance, those things he feels
and knows without needing to name them.

To amuse him, I lift a small boulder to my chest.
I heave it down, a firecracker snap next to the black
bellow of waves. Soon, we roll down
bigger stones, his hands beside mine, rock
after rock, trying our best to blur
one small edge of California.

Ezra, listen.
Listen, I say. He turns, his eyes
cloudless, sea-wide, waiting.

> *Las palabras*, the words.
> *Las olas*, waves.

I first tipped the bottle north, a brittle tube with your name wrapped around its neck, toward the empty temple just up the coast, toward the salt-bleached block ruins quarried from the interior, now nests for grey iguanas. Inch-high waves broke on my ribs. When I tipped the bottle into my hand I imagined the ashes would plume behind me like smoke from a thurible, but they just disappeared as my fist submerged, as they always will in water. On shore, a Yucatán cat, bright black, snatched a crab from the sand and carried it, legs whirring, into the tall grass, her dew-slicked belly mooning under her.

All my dreams end in a death.

I had to pick a place to begin, and that was the farthest from our home I'd ever been

> Clouds and their shadows
> make land here. Families of fish
> leap, shudder like coins,
> wishes. Are these enough to call
> a place and moment sacred?

—Toward Tulum, November

Metaphor Game

Scud clouds of starlings form and twist,
drop at wing's width onto the power lines
above us, chattering to the hum of the cables.
Cars thrum us with their exhaust.
Halfway to Fallbrook and a handoff
with his mom, Ezra stretches his legs
into long wobbly steps on the shoulder,
one slow foot thrown forward as far as it'll go.
He measures the world with his body,
in small or great lengths depending
on whatever he imagines himself to be,
dust-short or tree-tall.

He turns to me, my back against
the car window, my smoking hand curled
out of view. *Is it my turn?* he asks, grinning,
boy-stepping up the slope, and I nod.
I look for a simple object, some obvious tenor
he sees every day, easy to carve into words.
The sun, I offer, its paling circle a thumb's width
from the hilltops between us and the ocean.

He squints west, grinding his back teeth
like always. *Maybe a spark*, he asks,
about to hit the ground? Two starlings
shiver down to beads of ink on white space.
But isn't the sun, I ask back, *just a big spark,
another kind of fire?* He blows a raspberry.
I point to the lines, to the birds windwashing
themselves and each other. *What about those birds?*

He squints and sees them for the first time.
The dot dot dots you get, he taps the air,
when you forget something, and turns,
as if I've already lost him.

A part of the bottle tipped into a crack in the temple at the pyramid's peak, second tallest in the world. I carried your picture the 127 aching stairs up, the same picture I've warmed in my pocket since that night. The same picture I would lay on diner tables beside plates of untouched food and cups of cold coffee. The same picture I would rest on my knee while I wrote and hoped to wake one morning with you haloed in a fuzzy blanket beside me, just shaking off a long dream, as if all I needed to do was find where you were sleeping.

At Coba, I stood above the earth for the first time, above the green mirror of a jungle, thunderstorms blinking in the distance, *waters moved by a wind*. If I could believe you were there with me, were you there with me?

> Always, he glances up,
> soft grin filling the frame. Always,
> a blue stalactite, a drip
> of bubblegum ice cream, waits
> for his fist, for his next bite.

—Nohoch Mul

Zoo Tanka

What we thought were leaves,
scorched sun-white, shiver and fall—
moths trapped by daylight.

> His chest to the ground
> between cages, a boy whispers
> to ants trudging rocks,
> lint, food. He sees himself, now
> huge, but the world still wider.

Cat's feet strum the floor
all night, skipping stones, chasing
torn paper, dreamed wings.

> We are alone here.
> She lifts her head from the grass,
> the long shade, panting.
> She circles the pen, tongue dried
> white, darting, her teeth bloodless.

Junebugs long for a moon,
lost at a light, chasing
the whites of our faces.

> *See the bird?* a man
> asks his daughter next to us.
> A crane's blurred white head
> shakes a duckling to death. Down
> falls in clouds. *See it eating?*

How easy it is
to forget, then remember,
a snail shell snapping.

>The lioness turns
>circles for flat faces. Her jaws
>quake. The boy, once all
>roar and howl from my shoulders,
>quiets the glass with his cheek.

He lifts the shadow
dropped from the cat's mouth, dripping
feathers, neck gemmed red.

>The sky is quiet.
>He crumbles dry leaves into
>the pestle of his palm,
>into the gutter, such joy
>unmaking the things God made.

A part poured out at a bridge, the wrong bridge, off Pacific Coast Highway. Fine chalk banked like rivers in the seams of my palm. We came through here once, near here, when you were four and I was twenty. We ate apples on a cliff edge, watched a waterfall needle the ocean beneath an iron bridge. We threw rocks and boy-sized boulders down to hear them shatter between the waves.

Jenny and I searched for that bridge all day, drove from the pasture bluffs in the south to the jagged spit of Point Lobos. Wildfires had rearranged the redwoods on both sides of the 1, and bruised the road-split hills with soot. Still, I was sure you would remember. You'd know if the turnoff came before or after that stand of yurts on the left, the lightning-struck tree on the right.

In the end, I could only find some other bridge, some other creek clotting to the sea instead of falling into it, a sunblurred likeness of something I thought was real once.

> Out here, blue skin whips
> grey bone, sea on rock. Each crack
> hardens a memory
> into place, but not the one
> I came begging to find.

—Big Sur

4/14:   6:50 am: woke w/ headache, 2 Alleves
              —no food or water for 8 hours / ramen the night before

        10:00: headache not breaking, 2 Alleves
              —hot shower, neck massage, dimmed light, water, bagel

        12:30: not breaking, 2 Excedrins, car ride, nap

        1:15 pm: broken

4/15:   8:00 am: woke w/ headache, nausea, vomiting
              —no food or water for 7 hours previous
              —1 Excedrin + hot shower, cold compress on eyes
              —headache breaking

        9:00: shopping for Legos
              —headache returning
              —¼ buttered wheat toast, 2 eggs, 2 strips bacon

        5:30 pm: headache
              —tangerines, milk
              —1 Excedrin, broken

        8:30: vomiting
              —1 bite PBJ sandwich

        1 am: headache

        3: vomit, 1 Excedrin

        4:50: vomit

4/16:   7:30 am: woke w/ headache

        9:00: 2 Excedrins
              —neck massage, dimmed lights, cold compress
              —headache not breaking

        10:45: waiting for MRI
              —vomit in elevator, in potted plant
              —broken

Undated Photograph (PICU)

He is so thin here, balanced on a bed
in the PICU, his hand stretched out
in a pirate's hook, his chest candled
through brittle ribs, penumbras,
before dexamethasone. The windows flare,
clouding the narrow arch of his shoulders.
His cowlick twists off as it had since
the first cut, tumbling over the eye patch
like grass. You'd shave it down later.
He stares past the wall of the camera,
mouth ajar, about to crack a joke,
or whisper you one of his secret words.
After that first long seizure, he lost twenty pounds
in his sleep, while you circled the hospital at night,
smoking and calling anyone you could think of.
You read to him and prayed. You drew your knuckles
across the last smooth skin between torn tape
and electrode tabs. You learned how to read
the barbed lines of breath and green heartbeat.
You learned how to pronounce words
like *grand mal, glioblastoma
multiforme, palliative,*
and *inoperable*
without choking on them.

He's awake, at least, in the picture,
fished out of that starless water
and weeks of coma, so it must be May.
The steroids haven't begun yet to swell
him up, or wax his cheeks to soft moons,
so it must be early in May. His good eye
glimmers, sunken and serious, but still
the corners of his mouth are drawn
into the root of a tiny smile, a forming vowel.
The months-long headache must have broken.

To see him now is not enough: you need to hear.
If you could just hear the words again
that he almost speaks, that he spoke,
the beat and chuckle of that last joke,
the chime of his voice, you could remember
if this clear, caught second came before,
or after, you taught him how to say
cancer and not cry out.

A part dropped into the brackish stream too small to have a name, where my grandfather and I trapped bait crabs one summer. Mornings I followed him from the tea-soaked porch swing, past the bowl left on the step for a street cat, through the willows, between the ledge of the ditch and street, wind scolding our shoulders. He stopped when we found the mossy line, one end stretched tight into the creek's deepest pool, the other strung to the rebar in a stray jag of concrete. In three masterful draws my grandfather's huge sailor hands hauled up the wire box with a knot of crawling, clacking skeletons inside.

After he slopped the slate grey crabs onto the street, a dozen or so, *Stomp 'em quick*, he bellowed, *before they skitter*. I knew what we'd come to do, but it seemed so cruel then, the ball of his boot crushing their shells like dry leaves. Their eyes shimmered on stalks, and I cried. My eight-year old heart still believed in the innocence and immortality of all animals. Two beggar crabs groveled away from my feet. My grandfather floated over, barking, dragging his great heels, his hands, those shadows you never knew.

> Yes, all things pass: pets,
> parents, ourselves, our sons, not
> always in that order.

—Pascagoula

First Dream after Seizing

On the other side of the pulled blue curtain, paper crackles and vinyl creaks, sounds of one body lifting another onto a gurney. *What's seven plus twelve?* a man rumbles, breathless. The ER slows a second, then resumes beating. *Seven plus twelve, you can do this*, he repeats.

> *Nineteen,* a boy's voice cracks back, weak-lunged, too young for this place.

Good. Seven times twelve? the man asks.

> *Jeez. 84.*

Correctomundo. 84 divided by 3?

> Fingertips patter and scratch the paper sheet, thinking. *28,* the boy rings.

See? The man's throat unfists. *What's the largest mammal in the world?*

> *Blue whale.*

Largest fish?

> *Whale shark!*

Yes! Give me an animal with six legs.

> *Um, three quarters of a dead spider.*

See? You're still you. Now, squeeze my hand.
The hospital room clots like cooling glass, stops.
Squeeze my hand, the man says firmly.

I—I am, the boy's voice rattles, small, frightened.

It's okay, the man shushes. *It's okay— Just please squeeze my hand*, he repeats, over and over, quieter and quieter, fading into machine noise, droning out exactly how much one body can take, another can lose.

A part slung underhand into the small falls guttering from the big drop. I felt artless, clumsy, beside the smooth roll and tumble of endless water. You knew this place so well: where in winter we sunk our hips into snow and oak shade, in spring we chased lizards under rocks. We picnicked here one fall morning, a week after I began caregiving for Sylvia, a retired anthropologist who couldn't drive or carry coffee anymore. We moved our small life into her window-walled, ivy-draped attic, complete with grove rats tapping the glass at night, not where I imagined myself after grad school. But you would be safe there, I thought, while I cared for an old British woman and looked for writing work, a year and a month before your first headache.

Running, you kicked over a log to expose a million-strong nest of ladybugs, buzzing embers. Some flew, if they could. The rest crawled back over themselves looking for dark and the heat of other beetles. First, we used grass blades to touch the glimmering marrow of a bursted log, then a twig, then a finger. The red bugs tickled us with their dust-eating mouths, they swallowed our hands, a flame catching, and we played a game of staying still the longest. Of course, I let you win.

> He reaches for pebbles
> in a snow fed stream, something
> still under babble.

—Forest Falls

Dear Dad, Father, Sensei, Royal Kicker of Asses,

Happy Father's Day! I shall write you a letter: G. Now, since that is over, I shall prove to you how freakishly awesome you are as a friend, teacher, and Father.

All those years ago (11 years, 1 month, 6 days ago to be exact), you and my mother were in a hospital in Fontana when <Splap!> I came into your life. As most things that go splap are, I was a kind of ugly post fetus thing. It wasn't for a couple of months until I became a cute needy baby. As a baby, all I remember is sucking. And sleeping. Sucking and sleeping. Then came All-Hallows Eve, or Halloween. I was a bee, was I not?

OK, back to you. When I was 3 or so we play wrestled. You made me confident that I could kick the ass of anything. I was so happy!

Then I was six, waiting for Mom to come back from Seoul, I split my noggin open. Without you there, I would probably have given up hope. You were there, though, and I was OK.

Through thick and thin, groggy and smooth, red and yellow, you have taught me how to handle troublesome situations. Most recently Brain Tumors. (Oh no!) You have been a light through the indigenous tunnels of life, a book I could turn to when I needed help, and most importantly, you are the CREATOR!

Five.
Four.
Three.
Two.
One.
THANK YOU FOR BEING THE MOST KICK ASSINGEST DAD THAT HAS EVER SHOWN HIS SHINY FACE TO MANKIND!

Love, your son and growing post-fetus,

P.S. This is the best letter I have ever written. I hope you liked it.

Now, Someday

We came through here once, past
chains of rock-scarred, selfsame hills, past
the dusty squares that suddenly turn
to green lettuce like bottleglass, and back,
past yellowing honkytonks, taquerias, past
so many sheep huddled onto planks
of shade under a billboard.
I'm going to be a writer someday,
Ezra said, *but not as my main job.*
I was taking him up the mountain
to a camp for children with cancer
and other catastrophic ailments, a week
of wallet-making and pine cones, trees
shifting. Between his ankles,
his backpack flapped back, unzipped
to show an empty drawing pad
and a spray of unwritten letters, one
for each day, envelopes stamped
and addressed to each home.
Sailing his hand out onto the 74,
I asked him to name five amazing things
he hoped to do that week, the longest,
farthest we'd ever been apart.

What I remember now is Ezra
wanted to swim. He wanted to see other
kids carved from the same soft wood
as him, to float up in that stinging cool
and count the swaddled PICC lines,
the shaved heads and heads
furred with post-chemo lanugo,
steroid plumped cheeks or ribs
thinned to stacking stones by nausea,
tattooed radiation crosses,
white, half-knitted surgical lines,

and then, then, the whip welts,
blue stretch marks fanning across
all their trunks and limbs.

What I remember now is Ezra
being sent to the hospital the next day,
protocol for when his temperature ticked
over a hundred. I could hear him laughing
his unbroken laugh as I shuffled through
those shoe-smoothed, dustless hallways,
those hiss-shut doors. I could hear him
telling his nurses a dog and cat story
he'd written, or was going to write,
or imagined just that second.

What I remember now is Ezra
dry drowning in my arms.

A part buried in hot sand while Navy jets tore the air above us. Jenny watched a boat mark the horizon. She was your teacher. You loved her, and she loved you, your fearlessness in demanding to answer all the questions, the seismograph scrawl of your handwriting. The stash of dirt clods in your overflowing desk. All those middle names you kept giving yourself, until you were Ezra Phoenix Kabuto Jacob Scary Dary Zucchini Pickles Rainbow Robot Too Silly Basketball Jack Tomatohead Tomato Squirt Tomato Blowup Seventeen Chairs Quacking Umbrella Speed of Trees Flaco Taco Macho Pipi Garcia Chatterton.

Like me, Jenny had never lost anyone before. She knew enough, though, to look away when I wrote your name for the first time in months.

> Tonight, moths mandala
> around the skull of a bulb.
> Cats rest from the chase.
> Trees rest, mindless to their own
> median survival (in months).

—Coronado

I Can Take It

We had a trick for pain.
He would clench one or two of my fingers
when we saw the hot moment coming, whenever
we had the luxury of preparing ourselves.
Then, when the bandage ripped, the tube pulled
or the needle dug, he'd crush my fingers
as hard as his small hand could grind.
He'd bend them sideways, rolling
my knuckles like stones in a backflow.
We imagined the pain passing from its source
like gleaming dye, up through the estuaries
of his spine and heart, through his stronger arm
and back into the rock of my fist.
He truly wanted to hurt me, not to punish
me for letting the doctors claw at him,
but to keep from being alone
in the dry white spotlight of suffering.
I always lied a little, exaggerated
his strength, wincing and sweating, setting
my jaw to let him believe he could break me,
to show him he was not alone, to show him
how to let these things happen
and go on.

By the time he began forgetting to breathe,
all those stray cells damming the nerves,
he could only speak in hand signals—
a weak thumbs-up, a flipped bird, *eat, sleep, milk*.
His chest shuddered and stilled like sailcloth.
I held a Good Humor bar to his lips, read
him Psalms and Dogen. I made up a story
of two heroes who were caught in a storm
and blown to opposite shores of a black ocean.
They never stopped loving each other, searching,
carrying pictures of the lost one in their minds

and pockets. After many years, they found
each other again on some warm, unmapped
coast, so they knew then they would always
find each other. I tried to prepare him, to comfort
him by being strong enough to let this happen.
I didn't want him to fear for me too.
Imagine the pain coming from your heart,
up through your shoulder, down through
your arm, into your hand, and then my hand,
because they're the same, I told him, gasping.
Give me your pain, Ezra.
He grasped my fingers as hard as he could.
I can take it, I lied.

What I Said

In all the old stories, the best ones, there are two heroes who love each other completely. They could be brothers or best friends, a husband and a wife, or a father and a son.

In the beginning of the story, the two heroes have many adventures together. They find and tame dragons. They save villages. They try exotic foods. Their love is deeper and stronger and more proud than anything else in the world. Their hearts connect, and the companions believe, believe so completely, that they will always be together.

Then, of course, there is a storm. Black, stinging wind blows the heroes apart, to distant lands. Or it could be a villain that comes, a thief who snatches the younger one in the night. It could be a journey, like a vision quest, that only one soul may take at a time. So, they each must face their own separate adventures for a while, in their own cold, separate places.

This is only the middle of the story.

But, no matter what dangers they face alone, the heroes love each other and fight to find their way back. Their lonely quests and glories are great, but always they are moving back toward the one they love, a picture locked in the corner of each eye. It takes a long time for them to travel through their separate worlds, to see the things they see, but their hearts are good compasses. Because they love each other so much, they always know which way to face their feet. They know to keep walking, even through the night.

In the end, in all the best old stories, the two heroes do meet, usually from opposite ends of a long, warm shore, and they have their last, greatest adventures together. They are proud of all the distance they closed to hold each other again, all the tattered bridges they crossed alone and slobbering monsters they faced alone, but now, after so long, their bond is even stronger than before. They love each other more, which didn't seem possible when they were first saving just that small part of their world together.

Always, in the end, if two heroes love each other, they will meet again and will have their greatest adventures. They know then, in the end, that they were never really apart, because they loved each other so much. And when you love someone that much, as much as I love you now, and you love me, you will always carry them with you. You will never be alone, even in the darkest, farthest place, because I love you, and you don't have to be afraid.

You don't have to be afraid. You don't have to be afraid.

This is only the middle of our story.

A part blown into the grass in Sylvia's backyard, our backyard, where you wrote haiku one morning, stories, letters, anything else you could think of. I took pictures of you, bent into your thoughts, your hair finally beginning to darken over the radiation tattoos, your black cat, Violet, watching from the red gable of the balcony, leaves falling around us. You were just happy to see your words on a page again. Behind, the canal through the orange groves rushed off, only heavy enough to hear if we remembered to listen.

A woodpecker pecks.
Unaware, she keeps pecking
Until the tree falls.

Such a splendid sight…
Oh no! they've come to eat me!
EVIL PLATYPI!

You died in the northeast bedroom, with the one vine that kept growing in, working the window off its hinges no matter how far I cut it back. The morning before, Jenny, still just your teacher, brought books and cookies, none of us knowing how close we were.

The night of, the house brimmed with bodies, your mom and grandparents, friends who came to sit with you one last time. Violet, normally so shy, laid against your chest until you were cold, unmoved by the screaming in the room. The morning after, I folded your arms around your favorite stuffed animal, Commander Arson, an Argyle-sweatered koala. I folded a plush blue blanket around your shoulders and legs. Everyone else waited upstairs, to be spared this memory. I carried you to the coroner's gurney, rigor cracking, the last time I held you in that form, that body.

> *Then, the still warm sun*
> *his head traced in the pillow—*
> *God, he was just here.*

—Riverside

Condolences

How awful.
I'm so sorry for your loss.
I can't even imagine.
If you need anything, please don't
    hesitate to call.
Forgive me for asking.
How old / what of /
is, or was, he your only?
Oh, you're so strong.
He was so brave / so strong / a fighter / a saint, almost.
At least, he's in a better place now / at least he's at peace /
at least there's no more pain / at least / but then—
    You'll see him again one day.
You have to believe you'll see him again one day,
don't you? What's the point if— /
I think God must love some souls so much
he wants to keep them for himself / take them back
for himself / make them angels to watch over the rest of us. /
You know, how energy never dissipates, just transforms.
He was never quite of this world, was he?
He'd become perfect enough on this imperfect plane /
he was ready to transcend / be transformed.
You're handling it so well.
I would just die / fall apart / never wake up again.
My grandmother / grandfather / father / mother / brother / sister /
family spaniel died last year, but there's no name
    for parents who outlive their children.
Still, historically / biologically / as points on a cosmic timeline,
this has only recently become an unexpected event.
A tree will bend, but not break / will scar against wind.
You're still young.
After all wars people rebuild their homes
and churches from the bricks and wrack of the old.
You have a whole life ahead of you.
Try to hold on to the good times.

Remember only good things, what he was /
what he said / what he did / how he laughed
at his own jokes / remember the very last day
before he held his hands to his head.
But, won't it be better when you're able to forget?
The book says, to everything there is a season /
a reason / the Lord works in mysterious ways /
original sins / only begotten sons / Abraham
bowed and raised his knife hand / not for us
to know his will / but, still, David gnashed
his teeth, wept, and tore off his clothes
to save his son from fever, forever
lost to God's punishing thumb.
      Praise Jesus.
At least now you have something to write about.

A part spooned from the larger box to the lip of the bottle I carry with me always: angle and tap slowly to keep the ashes from spilling over into the bell of the sink, grey clouds on white, the little hailstones of shattered bones. I want to say what grief is. I want to cup my hand over the fragile matchburst of 'what grief is' and lift it to the corner of a page.

For example: grief is learning to carry another person's life on your back, his memories, his jokes, his updrawn eyebrows and cancer-whipped limbs, his hopes, how he saw himself at an age he never got to, and everything, everything, everything else that is another person's life. And one day, as you learn to carry his life, you realize you are also carrying your own life that was lost, how you saw yourself at an age he never got to, your memories, your hopes, jokes and so on. Grief is learning to carry the shifting, windsplit stones of two lives on your back, until, one day, you realize just how fully you've forgotten to live the life you have.

See? Not wrong, not quite right either. Grief is learning just how weak and fragile words are, memory is.

> I breathe him in, out;
> make my footsteps a mantra;
> remember his face,
> remember his voice, as if
> remembering changed anything.

—Kitchen Counter

First Dream of Becoming Ash

A boy lingers on a sunlit raft
of sidewalk, pigeon-toed. A man slips
back through the teeth of the glass doors,
swallowing the boy's fist with his own.
They step inside together. Cold air breaks
down the backs of their necks.

The boy looks up at the gallery around them,
from concrete littered with photographs of fires
to granite pedestals weighing down the walls
to glazed figures slumped over the huge cubes
and mandorlas of broken light behind them,
each piece the wick of its own candle.
The domed ceiling evokes smoke thinning
into sky. Somewhere, a zither glides
and panpipes murmur, for authenticity.

From his stillness in the center, the statues
of monks and nuns seem barely human, most
rigored into Lotus, lacquered brown, some
spilled onto their sides. The resin is smooth
where the robes covered, rough at an exposed
shoulder or the bowed match-head of a skull.
Some are more mounds of stick and shaped soil
than people. The boy counts them, as he does
when he's scared, seventeen human bodies abstracted
to fields of drapery with flourishes of burnt flesh
and dross: fingers and feet curled into birds' claws,
rinds of ears, fractures rippling from sockets
like crater glass, broken water.

He begs his father not to make him go
when the big knuckles nudge him forward,
gently, toward the centerpiece. The man grits
his teeth through a sob as he holds up his palms

to the largest, most painfully detailed statue,
certainly Thích Quảng Đức, burnt to death
in a gasoline fire, lips and skin erased cell
by cell in that last, most famous, act of prayer.

In the silkscreened photograph hanging above,
that won a Pulitzer in 1963, the bodhisattva
is perfectly still, his face calm as a riverrock
at the moment of eruption, consumption,
at the moment of form failing, his rosary
hidden in the flames, all watching, all
wailing from the other side of the street.
The boy remembers a kerosene lantern
he kicked over once camping with his father
in the redwoods. The trunk of Đức's car
is propped open, was never shut after
an unnamed monk lifted out the gas can, gently,
with full knowledge of what must come next.
Clavicles crossed by heat, the ragged skeleton
kept Buddha's pose, beautiful in a way.
The boy wonders how the sculptor captured
the body so realistically, the rupa embering,
as if still warm. Was he there, did he snap
photographs, scribble down last mantras?
Did he pour wax on the dead man in the street,
hoping the mold would cool before
someone from the sangha came to collect
Đức's bones, to burn them again, to sift them into
the curved script of their most sacred books?
In the straw nest of the ribs he can just find
the teacher's untouched heart, that would not
catch fire even in the crematory, that is said
now to grant miracles.

The man begins weeping loudly. *I'm sorry,*
he says. *So, so sorry,* hands outstretched
to pull the boy back, to turn him away.

The boy has never seen his father cry,
doesn't know what to do or say.
He can only count the *'so's*, the *'sorry's*,
the mantric breaths, the tears sparking
in white furrows. He can only offer
his hand for the man to catch as he falls.

July 27 3:41pm (Text)

Ezra:

Salooka? Meef foogle gobbin?
Who would win in a cubicle fight unarmed: a Klingon or a Wookie?

A part thumbed down into the knotted rootcrags, the handsome nebari of the 26 year old bonsaied sweetgum I bought when you died— a gesture, not a headstone. You always loved the stories of transformations, of mortals escaping their gods into the quiet and woundless musculature of a tree, or was it me that loved them, needed them?

I asked you once, after the seizures returned, once the cancer reclaimed its brief, breathy offering of hope, if there was anything you wanted me to do for you when the time came. You cocked an eyebrow, confused. You couldn't understand what I was afraid to say.

One of us thought of a tree: what it meant to have your form remade into limbs and bark and leaves that, if cared for and carried right, might outlive the both of us, which was the same as living forever.

So I ask you: how much ash can I seed this soil with, down into the ever coiling, spreading snakeball of roots, before *to honor* begins to mean *to poison?*

>   At night, the water
>   of my body joins with all
>   bodies of water,
>   for the moon to grasp at,
>   and the earth to be pushed by.

—Liquidambar

Things to Do Before I Can Kill Myself:

— ~~play World of Warcraft again~~, b/c that was our shared act

— ~~transcribe the texts out of your phone~~

— ~~open the box of ashes~~

— ~~transcribe your haikus~~

— ~~look at old pictures~~

— ~~grief group(s)~~

— ~~go back to the hospital, chocolates to the nurses on 4800, 2800~~

— write letters to Pascagoula, ~~to Blizzard~~, Elizabeth, ~~the grandparents~~, Eric, J + M, Jacquie, ~~Sylvia~~

— write a story about you (as an inventor? a robot? a spirit animal? yourself?)

— paint pictures for the boys who never knew you

— ~~do something unrequitedly romantic for someone~~ (Jenny)

— ~~have sex~~

— make arrangements for the animals

— remember you before cancer

Questions

When the fang tip of the instrument slips deep into your nose
and your eyes go white, when blood streams down to your mouth,
giving you a wet, red mustache, what more can I do than dab blood
and knuckle away tears? What more can I do than bar your arms,
hold your chin, and love you enough to let you suffer?

—

Where are you now?

Can I speak for you?

Did you call me *Dad* this morning?
Was it an echo, a memory rattled from the walls,
enough to get the timbre of your voice ringing in my skull,
to remind me I'm still your father, but not enough
to tell me how to be that now?

How can I be a father without trying to fit
some other child into the space of my wound?

Why does everything I write sound the same in my ear,
on the page? Is it that words are your only form now,
bloodless and hollow next to even the briefest flash of light
in which you are alive? Is it the ache of forgetting,
all the edges and contours of my memory wearing smooth
under grief, a million years of wind and water
polishing out a crack in my mind?

Is the recurring owl in the street significant,
lifting away from a puddle, into the air carved out by my headlights?
Is any totem, tree or bird or colony of rats, significant?

Why did you punch me in the head the night before the last night?
because you still could? because you knew what was coming?

How can I continue to live the way we lived?

        How can I devote myself to being funny, to believing the best
            will happen, when the worst has already happened?

Can I ever love another as well as I loved you?

                Can I ever love myself as well as you loved me?

Is there any graceful way to say your name to a stranger?

                  What did your stretch marks mean to you?
      tiger stripes? proud scars? just the color of your new skin,
         once you stopped seeing yourself as sick or well?
        What did your lost hair mean to you, your tape-torn
           arms, your sleep-weak legs? Can you show me
         that your mind persists somewhere, can you make me
              believe it, so I don't have to be so sad?

What do I do with all this hair, locks and locks
of your great hair shaved down before it shed
onto your pillow by the fistful?
If I were able to clone you one day, would I discover,
finally, how a soul grows from meager flesh?
Would I be allowed to live out this happy nightmare,
chasing the monster of your body?

                          Where are you now?

Did you know you were dying in that last week?
Did the moments blur into word soup? face gumbo?

                Were you with me today when I collapsed
          in front of your picture, crying, broom in hand?
          What are these gusts of emotion, with no thought
              or image, if not your breath in my ear?

Can I maintain this deliberateness of every action?
this constant strain of conscience, until I drink myself

to sleep? Did you feel me cut myself, the long draw
of a razor blade across my shoulder? Should I be ashamed?
Should I cut deeper?

                    When I imagine you beside me, will I ever stop
                        seeing you as cancer made you, still mastering
                  the proper technique to hold my elbows to stand,
                            to limp from the bed to the commode?
                          Your body, as it was, could never be here,
                        by the sea, the sand too soft, the sun too hard—
                but if I could make my eyes your eyes, my mind
                      your mind, could I feel you here, just once?

Will I ever mourn for your health, which was lost years ago?

                            How can I honor your life while I long
                        for the day of your death, while I long to lift
                    an ice cream to your lips, long to read you myth
                after myth, to feel you squeeze my hand, to know
                        what it was you cried out, terrified?

How can I honor your love of knowledge
when what I know now is so cruel:
that you are dead,
that you did everything right and are still dead,
that there is no wishing hard enough,
that I was never allowed to die in your place?

                                      Where are you now?

Who am I in this story?
Am I the Abraham who took his son and ran,
or would have if I could? Am I the Abraham
who talked you into death at the end, who pressed
the blade of my words to your skin while I waited
for a ram, for an angel to let you stay a little longer?
And now that you're gone, what offering can I give
that makes your death mean something,
other than my grief?

> Can I call this pain a cancer?
> Can I say that even as I grow accustomed
> to its place and hardness in my body,
> it shifts, and grows, imperceptibly?

Is this progress, every second
lengthening the silence between now
and the last time I heard your voice?
Do I even want it?

> What was the word we used to say
> to get you to lift your ass off the bed, to soften
> the shame of having to shit in a bedpan?
> Is this what I should fear most?
> that the hurt becomes its own memory,
> and you are lost forever, one word at a time?

What do you think of Jenny (Ms. Sherbon)?

> Is my way of grieving any better or healthier
> than anything else? than distracting myself?
> than barging headlong into a childless life?
> Is this me searching for a new way to fail you?

Were you a part of the world? Are you still?
Can you be a part of the world in such a short time?

> And yet, how can I still feel you on my fingertips?
> the little sink of your temples? the chemo-soft fuzz
> of your eyebrows pricked by a scar on the right, a mole
> on the left? your nose, which was my nose,
> subtly heroic, dimpled below the tip?
> You were real once,
> weren't you?

And yet, how can I write you
without making you an object? a character?
clay to be pulled on, or ash to be crushed together
with berries and palmed onto cave walls,

oil to be welled and burned? How can I write you
until you are gone already, almost forgotten,
some breathless third person?

                                          Where are you now?

What do you want for your birthday?

Aug 2 4:58pm (Text)

Ezra:

Some inventions of man we will never need: Mechanical widow washers, Lawn Ninjas, and sprinklers that can be mounted on a dog's back.

Self-Hypnosis

Go back.

Go back one moment,
to the first line of this poem.

Go back two moments,
past the first line of this poem.

Five moments, breathing in
the smell of smoke, somewhere a fire,
your finger clasped in a book. A breeze
turned like a voice beside you,
about to read this poem,
or write it.

Go back one hour.
You had your head in your hands,
or a child's fragile head was in your hands,
his tears pooling in your palm. Or else
you were happy, smiling at scraps
of overheard conversation, a bar joke,
a horse and a Rabbi, anything.

Go back one day.
It was raining, mud-grey all around you,
or it was hot, the sun a stone bearing down
on your neck with each blurred step,
sweat in your shoes, salt in your shirt,
or it was different.

Go back one year.
You were walking through cracked leaves
in a gutter, listening to their knucklebone rattle,
or you were standing behind a girl
in the supermarket, watching the crane

of her neck slip smooth like water
as she thumbed a magazine,
or you were other places.

Go back ten. You were sitting
on the poured stairs, coiling a strand
of hair back around two fingers as you do
when you want to write, trying to remember
the first time you saw crows and knew their names,
or you were standing behind a door, watching your wife
pour water on the baby in a white bathroom sink,
or you were other things.

Go back to the first time you saw crows
and knew them by their burnt metal colors.

Go back to the first dream of falling,
jerking awake to some truth suddenly
clear for a cold long breath. Go back
to the first dream in which you saw outside
yourself, first dream of music
where it shouldn't be, in the street,
in your chest, your slapped skin
and singing joints, first dream
of wolves, first dream of fire, first
dream screaming, first dream
in which you realized anyone could fit
into anyone else's body.

Go back to the first time you heard crows,
and knew them by their scratched glass voices.

Go back to the first girl you ever loved,
first boy you ever loved.

Go back to the first time you felt naked,
first cigarette, the hot half-breath
of it, first car crash and house-burning,
first bad haircut, first good haircut,
first dirty word or thought, and how
great it was to say or think, first black eye
or broken bone, first time you tasted your own
blood, first time you saw your own blood,
the first time you knew that all animals die.

Go back until you find
the first thing, the first thought, the first bright
plume and flash that became a part of you.

First thing: chasing grasshoppers
through tall brown grass, a dust-filled wind
on all sides of you. They clutch the dry stalks,
swaying in sunlight and waiting for you to touch
the green paper of their wings
before they fly.

First thing: you are held against
the pale moon of a breast, shadows spilling
out behind the curve. A huge finger
dots the tip of your nose
with a poke.

Go back to the brink.
Go back into that last brief firelight
that flung shapes on cave walls.
Your cheeks waver. Kneel, slither
across the broken floor. Find a place
where the blackness hems, breaks,
the cracked edge of a life you never lived.

Go back until half of your body is light,
and half of your body is dark.

Go back until all of you is dark.

Rest.

Aug 2 8:15pm (Text)

Ezra:

Also, the purple nurple alarm clock, vacuum tissues, and the caveman club spatula…

South Wichita Safeway

The first time my mother left me home,
Mount St. Helens exploded.
She crowded around a little grey radio
at the checkout, a milk bottle sweating
against her ribs, the butcher behind her
towing a cloud of Camel smoke,
beef fumes. She listened
while a reporter barked about lahars
and pyroclastic flows, blast magnitudes
and missing mountain men, his voice
bearded with static. The eruption scalped
its peak, the whole north rockface, an island
almost, shook out into the sky, bears and all.
She sighed and gasped, overwhelmed
by secondhand atrocity. She tried to imagine
a million trees snapped, blown sideways
in a sharp second, tried not to wait
for that avalanche to rush the city limits
and uproot every church, strip club
and slaughterhouse she knew.
How exciting it all was for a day,
how mildly disappointing when, by next
morning, the mountain's headwind of ash
had drifted only as far east as Boise
and Edmonton, heaped quietly on green
leaves, windowsills and woolen vagrants,
only a mid-May snowfall, just
another kind of winter.

A palmful, a larger measure toed into the dirt under the bent canopy of the back pomegranate, for afternoons we laid out in the tang of orange blossoms drifting off the groves, for nights we followed the lights of rats' eyes chewing the red globes, for home movies we made in this shade, for Hide-and-Seek, for birthday parties with brain-shaped piñatas, for your wake, for our home.

Jenny and I will be married today. Help me find the right words, Ezra, and strength enough to leave this place.

>   Finally, black buds
>   fatten and crack, to say, *This tree*
>   *can still grow, take wounds.*

—Pomegranate Tree, June

Young Couple

Sandals in hand, a man and a woman
joined together to watch the ocean lick
its lips, clack its teeth, then decided to find a cave

to lie in. They turned to the cliffs
upshore, cracking loam like snow under
their hot heels, eyes out for the right gully or hollow,

and when they found it, she bowed
to enter. He crawled in on rough knees past
scattered deer pellets and a rock that might be bone. The walls

pushed against their palms, raw
as marble as they shivered off their clothes,
made a nest on the dirt floor, lowered themselves, and, hands

clasped, gazed up at the bare ceiling.
Let us be bison, they said. *Let us be horses,*
lions, thick-necked aurochs and the thin men hunting them,

spears drawn. Let us be red
and yellow ochre. Let us be cochineal,
hematite, rose madder, charcoal. Let us be the outlines of bodies,

pigment blown through
hollowed bones against the backs
of our hands, to make a void that lasts forever, they sang,
their flesh chipping against itself,
sparking in the dark.

A part scattered into the headwind gnawing the bow-pulpit of our tour boat. There was the skyward coast. There, beneath the horizon, were volcanoes making new land every day. There was my wife with a camera for a face. For a few hours, I didn't think of you, until I stood on the ocean and wasn't afraid.

>   Parapeted on hips,
>   a boy gleams at me across
>   the deck, happy, fragile.

—Na'Pali

Flagstaff

So we stand where the dry lawn stops, boys being boys
throwing rocks at grasshoppers on the wall of the Navajo house.
We fight over who throws hardest, farthest, whose eye is deadest.
One bug suns itself by the screen, unfurls its light-worn wings.
We roll smooth stones across fingertips, imagining leather
stitches, taking aim through a funnel of red dust.

Then we throw, on three. The grasshopper shutters its belly
in a black husk. Four stones clap plaster, cluster under the window.
A jump cut, a trick of the eye, something suddenly transformed
in the whole of its body and the way the world knows it: a spattered
animal, its tar gut spilled out, black stars on white. The body peels
into the weeds, one thorned leg pinned and kicking.

Then we hoot and tussle over who got the kill. The leg jolts,
tied by a wet string of muscle at the joint. One of us watches while
the others argue, click their tongues. Blue sparks must be looping
in the leg, furious, the instinct to leap still burning in what little flesh
remains. One of us taps his sneakers in the dirt, inching away
as he wonders just how long a thing takes to be still.

Then we jump back when the Navajo lady bursts out
the front door with a belt in her hand, her rum crumpled braids
screwing off like branches, her dry brown fists swinging circles.
One of us, smaller, standing away from the rest, cries out
when she catches his collar, hot words on his neck
as she lifts the leather.

Then we scatter.
We come together again in a cloud.
We cuss down the houses.

A part funneled into an empty hotel shampoo bottle. Jenny and I paddled hard and clumsy down the Wailua River, stumped over footworn logs and outcroppings, through calf-deep, ferrous red mud, through drifts of mosquitoes, into the shallow pool, the deep pool, the stinging falls.

There, in the dark beating of the waterfall, I pulled the bottle from my pocket and unscrewed the cap; ashes welled invisibly out of my hand, as they will in water, became silt, sand, just another ghost rushing to the ocean.

> Father, mother, child
> nudists claim their bend of bank
> with our averted eyes.

—Secret Falls

Snabu

after my dad

We say *F.*
F-er.
F-ing.
F-ing S.
Shoot.
Darn.
Gosh darn it— but never *God damn it*
        because we don't speak for Him.
Damn is OK— but only if the skin breaks.
Dang.
Dagnabbit.
Friggle nabbit.
Crabble dabbit.
Ticked.
Pissed.
P.O.ed.
We say poop.
Crap.
Dog crap.
Horse crap.
Bull crap.
Horse shit— but only when family is involved.
Piece of crap, for when there are moving parts.
P.O.S., for when the parts won't move.
We don't say *suck* in this family,
        because just *who* is sucking *what?*
Bloop.
Blooping son of a bloop.
Situation Normal All Blooped Up.
Furshlugganner.
You can say *mother*— but only if the dog breaks
        down the street, if the hammer sways
                thumbward, if swerving for your life.
Or *motherfucker*— but only if the blood won't stop.

A part sighed out on the Old Pali Highway, at the cliff of falling warriors, those 400 skulls dashed along the rockheads. Someone told me once my grandfather worked this road with a G.I. crew during the war, after the attack on Pearl Harbor, that it kept him safe for a while. True or not, I can just see him, a projectionist in peacetime, a quiet man, leveling koa trees with a two-headed axe in one hand, pouring asphalt onto the windward face of the mountain with the other, lucky enough to die an old man.

> Cicadas: the porch
> swing sways on its screw eyes. White-
> ribbed, bristled, he guards
> crumbs of egg left on the last
> step for a street cat weeks gone.

—Nu'uanu Pali

Armadillo

Almost to Louisiana, an oil fire
leapt up white, gnashing out of a field east
of the road. I could see a swarm of tiny men
and shovels circling the well, shaking, just visible
beneath the dark swells of smoke and cloud
rolling low in the afternoon light.

The U-Haul's cracked plastic dash rattled
out songs I hadn't heard for years, raspy notes
split by the grind and tick of the wiper blade.
Above me, three turkey vultures spun on an axis,
kite-strung to a stone, their heads bald and red
as matches, even at this distance.

An armadillo lay dead on the shoulder, a crushed
husk, the first one I'd seen since I was nine, driving
with my grandfather through some hot Mississippi
bayou. When I was young, I would press my temple
to the cool slab of the back window, tallying
each animal I saw scratched black onto the road.
I hoped to hold them all in my head, to mourn
as a magnitude if I could, always failing.

A thunderhead of blowflies lifted quietly
from the carcass as I drove past,
toward the waiting wall of ash, forgetting
one thing, remembering another.

A part flecked into the highest crook of the stream that knots the trees above the cemetery. Coin-scaled koi thought you were food, chawed the surface with their silently moaning mouths. An ancient bell gonged in the valley for good luck. You would have liked this place, curious as you were about Buddhism, Christianity, and anything else we could think of to make you less afraid, if only for a night.

Inside the temple, I lit incense and stood a sprig in the tray of sand before the massive tin Buddha. Jenny waited at the doorway. A Japanese tourist knelt beside me, shoes in his hand, forehead to the cool concrete. I watched him pray, wondering what your soul would look like, its weight in my hand, if I should take my shoes off.

> I try to believe
> souls linger, speak, sing. But what
> might be wind, must be.

—Byodo-In Temple

Grandpa

He fingers the rosary of the rebreather
hose, panics and paws the mask
with his gaunt palms, his dishwater skin.
They do that sometimes, I tell my mother.
I try to sound knowing and gentle, the only
one in the house who has witnessed a death.
It's part of the timeline.

The blanket on his chest slows, stops,
22 beats to a breath. The box of his mouth
opens and shuts. He grips at the clear hose
like he's reining a horse, greenbreaking
a young thing, remembering all
the Missouri colts he birthed, and bathed,
and shoed, and let out into the back field
to leap against the fence he built,
or fold their legs in the shadow
of the barn he built.
Relax, he'd call as we loped down
the long driveway, my backbone
stilting from the smooth worn saddle.
She knows where to go.

I count 37 to the gasp,
then his hands slack almost completely,
trusting the mare of his flesh
to bear him the rest of the way.

A part left on the trail to Manoa Falls, in a stand of bamboo whose leaves rattle like rain whenever a breeze hits. This is the jungle from *Lost* and *Raiders of the Lost Ark,* old sets and polar bear cages rusting in a gully behind the trailhead. Each green trunk, each red bulb of ginger, each blue shred of sky through the canopy is a moment, a shutter click, a flicker of TV light from my childhood, or yours.

I wish I could have understood you at the end, when your breathing slowed to tiny, deliberate gasps, threads of glass spinning into the air above you. You tried to call out, your eyes begging me to understand what your lungs were too weak to press into words. If I knew what you wanted to say, could I have held on to that moment longer, tighter, instead of learning that nothing is unforgettable?

> Faces flat, round as coins
> smile as if they see me, kneeling
> trailside, knees muddy.

—Manoa

Custer's Last Haircut

1876

Libbie saw it weeks before, in a vision—
        Smoke. Prairie grass
slicked red. Horse and rider piled together
like brass-buttoned kindling. Carrion birds
carving the air. Her husband as Saint Sebastian,
pierced by seven arrows to the feather.
He knelt, bound before a half-moon of heathens.
His beautiful face, of course, was unmoved
as they gathered scalps from the pale bodies.
It was unmoved, glacial, when the shadow
behind him became a bear, became a man
clutching his hair in one barbed fist,
that most famous golden shock in the Union,
and a knife appeared against his pate.
In one silent move, the stone blade
slipped through skin, his scalp pulled back
on a crown of moon-colored bone—
        and she woke gasping.
George woke with her, his ivory sword
parting a shadow. Libbie wept at his feet,
at the apparition of her great love lost.
So the next day she sheared his mane
and begged him to keep it low, convinced
this was God's warning and God's will.
She even shaved his handlebar mustache.
She was a very religious woman.

1990

Ten years old I knew no stories, stalking
wild donkeys from the crest of the battlefield,
listening to the Little Bighorn rush away
from snorting crowds of German tourists.

Later I heard that Custer kept knucklebones
from Washita in his bullet pouch, boiled smooth,
that after the massacre Elizabeth Bacon Custer
spent the next fifty years of her life defending
his heroism, his good name, what with the glory
given those fools at the Alamo. Later I learned
the stand of oak trees by the river still carried
bullets in their limbs, knife digs, arrowheads,
a hundred years of once-lovers,
and, somewhere, 'Custer's an Asshole'.

But I knew enough then
to tiptoe toward the herd of fat ponies
as they searched for shade,
my fists full of long soft blades
pulled from a suddenly balding hill.
I knew enough to whisper as I held
out my hands to their round noses,
to keep silent when one accepted
        my gift of grass.

A part dissolved at Hanauma, into the cove where I lost my wedding ring on the last day. It slipped off my finger near the entrance to the Keyhole, where the harsh reef stabs out at low tide. My neck and shoulders blistered somersaulting in that one spot, running my face along the frantic bottom until my mask filled. Underwater, I thought to ask you to guide the ring back to me, glinting in a sandbank, or to someone else at least. A ring is nothing without a finger to wrap around, and what is prayer without a little haggling?

I tried not to take the loss as an omen, to think that somehow I might have foreseen this life if I'd only been more afraid.

> All things are not signs.
> A gull falls, silent. The sea
> takes without asking.

—Keyhole

Negligent Avocadicide

Isn't there tragedy enough
for a poem in the small passing
of an avocado, its meat waxed black
and thready around the skull
of the seed, lifted too late
from the gutter of the basket?
I was searching for a smell.

I chose that fruit with every hope,
had it brought from Hemet or Chile
to sit cubed in tortilla soup
or spun into rich spinach drinks
as I have brought pineapples from Thailand,
red bells from Holland, bananas from Ecuador
to play other parts in other dreams,
but I did none of those things
because I was tired.

Isn't there emotion enough for art
in a mealing honeydew, the sudden snuff
of sour dribbling from the drills in a coconut,
yellowheaded broccoli crowns, garlic bulbs
shrunk in chaff, weeping grapes, an onion sat
in its own milk, lettuce leaves like wet newsprint,
plum-eyed potatoes, tomatoes turned soft
on their faces, and mouthfuls of pearflesh,
spots and all, turned to sand on my tongue?

Yes, there are only so many hours
on the counter, so much heat and humidity
a body can take. I know the world withers
in parts and pieces, pome by pome,
each in its own way and moment, and yet
I always trick myself into believing
there's more time, there's life left.

Then I reach for a week-old avocado,
hard when I picked it. The skin gives
in under my thumb. Then I drive a knife
through the rind, down the middle,
split around the pit, and for a second
I imagine Cain, hands wet, so confused
as he searches for the fault in his offering,
the fruits of his soil and bent back
sitting spoiled in a hot heap on the table,
to which the Lord had not respect.

A part placed under a window of the library where I work, walls colored and lined with the spines of children's books. Each day, I try not to forget you. I make lists of what not to forget: reading to you as a baby, as a boy, in all your sick beds. That every bath you took was a wrestle, a race, but you loved gas station car washes. The way your eyes wandered, one stuck while the other tried to find itself. Your mumble, your muzzled smile. The way you'd slip a soft cuss into conversation or issue grand decrees on junk food and videogames. The way you'd echo the last halves of sentences, *the last halves of sentences*. I forgot today was your birthday, then remembered, and collapsed in the stacks.

You would have been fifteen, instead of twelve years and 92 days old.

    Birds break their own necks
    in here, lost in the books, cracked
    on skies of windows.

—Library, July 20th

Lucky

I get what I can before Ismael comes
with the telltale gnarl of the big diesel:
books I haven't read and tools I don't use
from the trunk, jumpers, jack, sloshing bottles
of antifreeze, change, the little jaundiced
eye of a Sacajawea dollar,
dog collars, water bowls, dry diapers, years
old bits of paper— how could I carry
and forget so much for so long, so far?

Dashboard dust crests against my fingertips,
snags the catch in my throat. I find and fold
atlases into a box of loose crib parts,
old roads worn soft, the lines gnawed white by wind.
The block cracked at sixty, vents bleeding heat
into the cabin with the sick rattle
of a machine shaking itself to death.
I unravel the graduation tassel
from the rearview mirror, cup the sunworn
threads still gilt on the shade side, that has swung
beneath each of my mirrors, eighteen on.

The guttural chug of the tow truck caroms
down the street, a garbage truck perhaps. All
that's left is trash, a torn leash, straw wrappers,
receipts, leaves and sticks, a penny ambered
to the well of a cup holder. One last
time I reach deep beneath the seats, and nudge
a small wooden chest caught between crossbars,
under the passenger, hearts sawed in sweet
cedar. Shaken free, the box is lighter
than I remember, than her body was.
Nearer, the truck coughs to a light, hisses.

To lift the lid is to remind myself
what we become: silk roses, a dented dog tag,
crisp paper prayers to Saint Francis, a bag
full of ashes and what feels like broken glass,
slipped with love back into a short-lived dark.

A part shook into the lavender bush where your old cat Violet likes to curl down, attended by clouds of humming bees, her tail a ticking metronome. She likes to warm herself on the red dirt. Once, she warmed herself in the lee of your chest as the heat left. Once, as I lifted a knife to my shoulder to widen a scar started the day before, Violet leapt from the bed to my back, drawing blood. I was shocked, angry for a second, my hand wrapped huge around her neck as I pulled her off. Then, I was struck by a deep sense of being watched. Not cared for at all, but cared about, maybe. I wondered if it was possible you leapt into her when you died. She stayed with you as long as I did.

Eventually, she'll yawn, and stalk off to hunt hummingbirds. Eventually, I'll find a precious green carcass left as a gift by my bed.

> I almost don't see,
> under threaded red feathers,
> small flickering breath,
> and wings waiting to dive out
> of the flower of my fists.

—Hillside

Folk Medicine

for Sylvia and her mother

For a nosebleed: drop
something cold, a coin or key,
the length of your back.

Wicked lumbago
needs brown paper ironed hot,
pressed into the small.

To improve eyesight,
pierce your ears and get some gold.
Silver does nothing.

Rheumatism: carry
a young spud in your pocket.
Or soak in Epsom.

Sore throat: tie a wool
stocking round your neck; Father's
sweaty sock will do.

Linseed, lime for burns.
Boiled onion poultice for ears.
Bread poultice for boils.

Bluebag for bee stings.
Warm cow dung for carbuncle,
or draw the devil

out with a hot glass.
Rub butter on a bumped head,
fig leaf on a bruise.

In case of a cut,
a little whiskey leeches rust.
It's good to let dogs

lick an open wound,
but only those you know well,
not some thin-boned stray.

Next, to clot the cut,
use cobwebs, fresh cigar ash—
in a pinch, sugar.

Egg water causes warts,
and touching toads. Spin horsehair
around your finger,

or daub with sow thistle.
If that cure fails, steal a piece
of meat. Rub the wart

into the cold chop.
Bury it in the garden.
Tell no one. The flesh

and the wart decay
together. Some say you need
a dead cat. Jabber—

any meat will do.
No, what we make we make in
burial, in hiding.

A part dropped into a pit I dug at the base of the young pepper tree on the back hill. Morning fog rolled down from the baseball fields, from the air base, from the veterans' cemetery, thick enough to wet my hair as I cupped away soil. More hummingbirds, small spirits, shivered in and out of the milky distance.

This is my home now. I beg you, Ezra. Haunt me here, at least in dreams.

> I know somewhere, past
> the cold fog swallowing trees,
> houses, hills are burning.

—Reveille

First Dream of Kinship

Remember this, then.
There is a girl at the edge
of town, window jimmied, slipping
lumps of scrambled egg and hard toast
out onto the damp side of the sill.

Morning fog's bitten off all
but the nearest branches of the family
sycamore, and the family of crows
living there, chittering, churning
the clouds with their wings.

There's a line of objects laid neatly
along the dry side of the windowsill:
a pebble, a paper clip, can tabs, beachglass,
earrings, buttons, a cat's broken femur,
the silver half of a heart.

She waits with her nosetip cold
to the pane, quietly breathing herself
into the swirl of an old man's beard,
until one by one, dewhooded
and coin-eyed, the crows come

clutching gifts, offering trade.

A part for a moment of thinking I know what I want most, palmed through the rye at the Festival of Books, listening to storytellers and poets try to lilt over the rolling gravel of crowds in motion. On the other side of the pavilion, a trumpet swirled into an upturned hat. Jenny guarded half of a green bench, resting her knees, counting each pregnant belly in the crowd.

> The whole ride she says
> nothing. Crows still on the lines,
> waiting to scatter.

—Los Angeles

Love to All, S~

I read her the Bogotá letters she mailed to Mother
in 1960. She stares up at me, sheeted in her sour midden,
eyes blinking like blown coal, aching to remember
her own life, her fingers on the Underwood,
to see herself again in dig coats and dusty hotel mirrors,
that Berkeley-trained gringa, that child exile of the Blitz,
far from home, as an anthropologist must always be.
She barks in a Yorkshire accent whenever I mispronounce
a township, *Ramiriquí, Sopó, Facatativá* gumming in my mouth
like dry bread. I want to read her face, and follow the recognition
as her gin blossomed forehead tightens, slacks to the words
greying in the cumulus of my voice.

>*You are 26 years old, Sylvia, broad shouldered and sandy-haired,*
>*crawling through a mountain to the Salt Cathedral at Zipaquirá,*
>*the altar a block of the purest salt you've ever seen.*
>*You are counting bullet holes in the wall of the Museo Nacional,*
>*where firing squads did their daily business for a century.*
>*Frantically, you bail mud from the dolmens in the dam's path,*
>*Guatavita's shoreline creeping toward the find of your career.*
>*You shoo Penny off the balcony. He keeps gnawing*
>*down geranium limbs, eating the fuchsia.*
>*Eduardo throws a sack over a comadreja, a weasel*
>*in the attic, and skewers it with a pitchfork.*
>*You take notes while the chicken thief's shrieks fill the fields.*
>*People ask aloud, but quietly, when Las Violencias are coming back.*
>*Appearances of the Virgin follow bodies of previously sacred water.*
>*One night a government truck plays "The Twist" on a loop,*
>*you dance, dance in the plaza with the local torero, drunk,*
>*throwing back black coffee whenever you float past your table.*
>*This is you, Sylvia, waving from a VW Bug at the head*
>*of a slow parade of threshers and pack mules to the Livestock Fair,*
>*skinny bullfighter for a Prince Charming, rockets blazing, blurring*
>*overhead, wrangled somehow into this, your life's version*
>*of a fairy tale you once imagined as a child.*

Her face is full finally, not smiling, but smooth as a windbellied sail.
A stray patient, doubled over, rolls in from the hallway dragging
a doll by its smudged ankle. The woman's tongue hangs past her lips
and untoothed jaw, jutting in and out, at once ghostlike and mechanical.
She shuffles her wheelchair to the other bed and lifts her head just
enough to hold a blanket over the baby's face. She whispers, *If she dies,
she dies,* again, again, with just a trace of Alabama upglide.
I press the call light.

Sylvia clutches my wrist when I stand to leave. I won't tell
her where I'm going. I can't risk telling her where she is now
and watch fifty years of dust cross her face.
So I say, *I love you,* the leaves of her hands and shoulders
trembling, and she says, *I love you, Allen,*
who died before I was born.

A part, a palmful, heaved into the blue stars of jacaranda flowers scattered outside the hospital, a larger measure for my wife's first son, my second, the brother you will be, or would have been.

    Then the heart flickers,
    a winding flame, a bird's eye,
    A boy, she echoes.

—Ultrasound

A Love Poem
for Jenny

What did you see in there? you asked later,
mermaid red hair floating past my pillow.
I saw the way we leaned to kiss, how we
made cairns of our cold feet, spun up shivers
from still places in our bodies, then fell asleep.
Queen of noses, Vitruvian wife, worried
nursemaid to the world's most delicate dog,
remembrist of first things, spontaneous
cupcake baker, teacher of small children,
teacher of just one unforgotten child—
I thought, What a mother you'll make, Jenny.

I saw too how your fear would ache into
panic, beebuzzed by unchecked burners, un-
pulled doors, forever waiting for a beltfall,
for some fate you might, should have seen coming:
scuffed heels, uncoastered cups, germs or burglars.
So many days you sat in the driveway,
eyes shaking, willing yourself: Turn the key.

Yet, somehow, you loved me enough to risk
my inevitable tremors of grieving.
Somehow, hours ago, weeks pregnant, you leapt
into the shower fully clothed, new shoes
sopping, mascara bruising the porcelain,
to catch me, collapsed by a memory.

I saw you, the mother you've always been,
the family I never thought I'd have again.

A part thrown into the creeping Pacific, the sun a coal cooling between my thumb and finger. Brown pelicans skimmed overhead, not flocking together, but not alone either. Jenny sat on slag by the road, because her belly and ankles couldn't make it down the slope of ovoid rocks to the water. She was not with me, but I was not alone.

>   Falling in the dark,
>   we forget where we are, who,
>   until our hands touch.

—North Ponto

Sand

Shudder and drop like water.
Shape yourself into a stone,
but be ready to abandon that form
in any hard wind.
Multiply by breaking apart.
Let waves rasp over, gnaw
you down into finer, sharper
mirrors of the pebble
or mountain that was once
here. Wait. Drift
and bank against my feet,
pressed to the tideline by shivering
families, boys with red shoulders,
paper-skinned ladies tucked
into the pages of a mystery.
After the wave, show me splinters
of pink conch and fish rib
settling in my shadow.

A little girl begs her father to bury her.
Once he digs, swallow her, but only
to the neck. Let him lay her in the cool
manger of your upturned body, mother of glass.
Let her feel your long-memoried weight
on her chest and thin limbs, wiggling
her fingers up like worms. Let her head
roll back in your geologic arms
that take granite, plastic, quartz, feldspar, teeth,
salt, boat lumber, old photographs,
every brittle thing that can be lost
and gristed into more of you.

Watch her. Wait for her
to laugh, or sleep.
I hope to be so ready.

A part breathed out from the highest branches I could climb, into the air around the great tentacled fig tree you fell from when you were seven. I'm too out of shape now to match your highest point, those thrilling limbs, but I found a spot to rest and remember. I ran my fingers along the trunk, dangerously smooth for climbing. You must have realized this too, too late. There, you hurled yourself onto a limb with your proud half-smile, your laugh, your blue eyes so sure that nothing bad would ever happen, just before the earth looped your ankle and pulled back.

Summer heat sucked my skin close even with a brisk wind. Ants searched the backs of my hands for salt. I brought Jenny here first. Two skinny college students were necking sloppily in the distance, on the bench where we unwrapped sandwiches and traded sad secrets, inching our bodies closer together.

You would have been sixteen today, instead of twelve years and 92 days old.

> If I said before
> that his eyes would brim over
> when he laughed, or cried,
> that they seemed to gather light,
> warmth, and give it, I forget.

—Fig Grove, July 20th

A Story I Remembered this Morning after Finding the Body Of a Lizard I Ran Over with the Big Can

In the story, she's skipping home from Sunday
school, her pretty, pressed Quaker dress gusting
against ribs, collarbone, her yellow hair a comet tail.
A moving spot, a tiny lizard on the sidewalk,
darts under her foot. She stops, mid-step.
It stops, stunned still in the patent leather
shadow of her shoe balanced overhead.
When she leans her weight to step over,
the thing follows her foot shade to shade,
and as she tilts her body back it always finds a way
to slip beneath her. Her other leg starts to sting,
so she jumps, it jumps, and somehow the whip
of its tail catches her heel, smashed part pinned
to the sidewalk on a coin of blood.
The lizard twists, strung down by its own flesh,
and she, in a panic, young girl, that never wanted
to hurt anything smaller than herself, stamps
hard on its head and runs home crying.

In the story, I think of a girl wrestling
with her own divinity, an inkling of her size
in the skies of so many small beasts.
I think of God standing on one leg,
trying so hard not to crush us
as we shadowjump through innocence,
until we all nail our tails to the point
of some first mistake.

How we scurry, tiny-eyed, from one cool
place to another on the burning stone of our lives.
We never question the mountains that shelter
and cloud us, how they swing by a thread.

I think of those animals living in constant fear,
fear of starvation, fear of being ground to dust
by the pestle of that watchful eye,
and in our fear we stumble forward,
slapstick, into our next sin, the footfall
of the suffering we must deserve.

But, then, it's only the end
of the story that needs death
or God or panic. Before that,
she is blameless, even comical,
some sweet girl holding her foot in the air
forever, wind sweeping through
her knees, sunlight warm on the wings
of her arms, trying not to
break the earth by walking on it.

A part spilled off the blade of my palm into the shower stall of the room where your brother was born. In the bed at the other end, Jenny sang to him as he nodded, a milksong, calling from her body to her breast to his body. I forgot how easy it is to make up a song for a newborn, that instinct to swaddle each word with a note.

Ashes clumped on the tile. The shower stream was too thin to wash them down. As I knelt to sweep the hard flecks, the splintered glass of your skin and hair and clothes and bone into the drain, I tried to keep my mind in the room with my wife and new boy, the breezing bell of her voice. What else could I remember about babies, had I forgotten about babies, about you, Ezra, first son? Your pink-gummed cry; your nose, same as mine, same as Samuel's; the fine white down on your skin; how fragile your body was in the beginning, that tangle of weak neck muscles and soft spots, and the little seed of a tumor just beginning its ten year sleep?

I tried not to think of how fragile your body was in the end.

Over my shoulder, Jenny and the baby closed their eyes, knowing I'd keep watch.

> His chest on my chest
> rises softly, recedes, my breath
> a swell to sail on,
> my mind squalling from the son
> I lost to the son I might.

—Labor & Delivery

First Dream in Which the Wind Speaks for Someone Who Isn't There

Salt the deep pot first.
In half dark tramp down garlic
with the boot-heel flat of a knife,
careful to keep the ruckus
of husks from disturbing them.
Your son felt wind rush over
him for the first time today.
Your wife clutched him under
her chin, and a slick chill
chapped his ears, his cheeks,
the backs of his hands, even as
he giggled into the rumbling howl,
even as his breath leapt out
to join the flocks of air
rocking the leaves, his hair,
        his body below.

Spin a loop and whorl
of cream into the shallow pot
as he curls into the curve
of her breast and arms, roots
raveling, snores ringing together.
Smooth the red sauce pink.
Creep across the floor,
trim the pale ends
of asparagus, wash and cook
and watch trees shudder
soundlessly in the dark outside,
as if to mouth words.
Then, you can scatter stars
by soft handfuls into the window
above their waiting heads.
You can give them a little
        light to wake to.

Two parts, two palmfuls puffed into the uprush where Samuel first saw the ocean, first tasted salt, first crawled over his name and yours carved in wet sand by the spear tips of our fingers.

Close your fist, I told Jenny as I poured into the cool chamber of her hands. She seemed to sense she was holding a portion of your blown glass body, cradling your atoms, your carbon like a fragile animal. *Wait for the wave to come in*. Samuel rested his cheek on her shoulder, curve gritting against curve, wind drawing down his eyelids.

When the swell came in, she hesitated, nervous, a shivering communicant. I only went ahead of her by accident. But on the next wave, ankles wet, she blew into the cool chamber of her hands. A gust took the ashes, held them up; we followed the shadow so long as they caught light.

> From my wall of arms
> he minds the ocean, always
> and never moving,
> close enough to salt his lips,
> far enough to rest the sky.

—North Ponto and a Year

Notes from the Life After

When I find quiet,
        frogs mumble under the streets.
Dogs haunt the orange groves.

Wind drags the limbs out,
        and me. I am bark to ants,
trying to recall.

Shadows churn and stretch
        across a screen. There: the spine,
eyebrows, hands folding.

Nature should not have
        moving things, she breathes, chin-deep.
A flying fish flies.

Inside, my wife sleeps.
        Inside her, my son sleeps, hushed.
Wait and watch for stars.

Let the sun settle,
        branch-broken, on his shoulders,
on his just-born skin.

A grasshopper leaps.
        The baby bawls in her arms,
her neck a cool stone.

Whiskers ring the sink.
        When he cries from his crib, I
comfort the mirror.

Slipping him between
        her knees, they are one body
again, in water.

I drift to my car,
	ragclouds huddled on housetops,
pretending to move.

We only borrow
	this world, these faces. A wave digs
little graves for my feet.

A palmful instead of a penny tossed into the fountain in the courtyard. The sound of falling water submerged the low roar of the particle accelerator under the building, that had made radiation viable, that could kill the smallest motes of brain with minimal backscatter. The closing growl of thunder in the parking lot submerged the sound of falling water. All the days and nights you were here, I must have smoked a thousand cigarettes between the cars, streetlamps for moons.

Inside, the storm played with the lights while I walked Jenny through the hospital, Samuel tucked into her hip. Of course, no one remembered me, and all the faces I remembered were worn down, thumb-smudged into unfamiliar people in equally garish nurses' scrubs. So I showed her other things.

This is the smell of the elevator that takes you to the cancer ward. This is the unwashed hair smell of the waiting room outside the PICU, where families sleep on torn down couches when they're told to go home. This is the weak bleach smell of the all-vegetarian cafeteria, which serves excellent meatless meatballs on Wednesdays.

The rain blacked us out. Jenny nursed the baby in that same wombish lactation closet where you came down from the steroid inhalations. Hopped up, eyes staggering, cancer cells abrading your nerves like glass dust, you said, *Dad, if you died, I just couldn't live anymore, anymore,* and paused, as if waiting for me to recite the next verse in our pact.

> I wake in the dark
> to his ghost shaking the air.
> His torn growl demands
> an answer: where was I?
> did I love him less by living?

—Children's Hospital

Bedtime Tanka

I read to the end,
though his eyes always loll closed
long before the wolf
scrapes grandmother's door. If I
stop, he shudders.
                So I don't.

For his birthday, we
give him a snap-jawed wolf, plush pigs,
to chase with, sleep with.
Brother Ezra gave you those,
we lie,
                as a family.

In weak light, his face
is his brother's. The shadow
he makes on my hand
cuts the same curve, the same hurt
he'll know too soon
                how to name.

A part, a vialful emptied onto the flat of Sylvia's coffin, a moment of white before the black of mourners' dirt spread over.

She loved you, and you loved her. After we met the first time, I took you for awful Chinese, which was our custom when happy. Your fortune read, *The kindness of a stranger will soon change your life*, and on that we decided to take her offer of what would be the last home you ever knew. Of course, you had to eat the paper of the fortune first to make it come true, which was our custom when we were happy.

After you died, I went to Sylvia at the nursing home each day, and she asked where you were, and I told her, and she moaned for you, day after day, week after week.

> We don't choose the lives
> we relive: she'll remember
> me when I walk in
> to dab the juice spilled down her chest,
> and forget when I touch her.

—Evergreen Memorial Park
& Mausoleum

Sphinx

1

When I was young

I gave a tangerine to a baby
to see what would happen.
At first, his mouth an unwound flower

of thin lips and throbbing gums,
he gnawed its curves for hours, savoring

the chill, the smooth of the skin, the fleshy
give, the sugared cells bursting inside.
Each day I pulled another fruit

from my pocket for him to teeth on, to slather,
to press against the stigma of his tongue

until he knew the scent, shape, and color
of a tangerine across a room,
and would leap angrily from my hip

whenever we passed the produce aisle.
Once, barely, a tooth broke in the night.

The next morning, mouthing a beautiful
mandarin, he tore the rind to the bitter white.

He screamed, of course, lips pulled in,
eyes wet, but bit again, then again, waiting
for the flash of sour, for the invisible

sliver of glass always aching to remind
us it was something else once.

2

A man and a woman become
a husband and a wife,
almost without realizing.
Every week he brings her a bag of fat
tangerines from a shack in the groves
by the veteran's cemetery.
Across the dinner table, he hands
her a mesh sack stretched wide
by gorgeous orange globes,
each bearing a winter's worth
of sunlight inside.

I love them,
she giggles.
I love the way
they spray sweetness
into my mouth
when I bite hard
with my front teeth.
I love the way
the segments look like ears,
tiny little babies' ears
I can eat,
she says.

He draws a knuckle
lightly along the moon edge
of the back of her arm.
You know that's how
cannibals talk,
right?

3

Somewhere, a magpie
caught the quick green glint of a knife blade,
even in all that snow.

I pulled three tangerines from the belly
of my pack and laid them in a sunbeam.

Somewhere, a black bear
never got cold or hungry enough to sleep,
a dazed beggar, wandering river to road.

She took one and he took one. I pierced
the bottom hollows with a soured fingertip.

Somewhere, a white labrador
leapt out of a moving truck bed, called out
by wind, and never touched the ground again.

Legs splayed in a snowpack, unsure, he dug two fingers
under the rind, juice bleeding past his knuckles.

Somewhere, a book
was left in the grass and sleet, to be undone
by mice, to be remade into shelter and food.

Remembering does nothing for the remembered.
He tucked the torn skins in a little white tomb.

Somewhere, a mountain
pretended to care about the people and animals,
even the trees, shivering on its back.

4

After the frost in the night a strange man
walks the rows of stones ahead of me,
enskyed by the deep morning fog, placing
tangerines on the markers. He bows to each.
His grey hand metronomes quietly
to the banana box propped on his right shoulder,
then down to the flat plane of a body and name,
or names, with a small, bright fruit,
the only sun they'll get today.

Following him, watching his dew-blurred arms
tend to hungry ghosts, I pass her by again,
as I often do, as I suddenly remembered
this morning it was her birthday last week.
I wet my knees on her scrap of grass and earth.
The tangerine on the stone sits carefully away
from the unmoving rivulets of her name,
what her job was, the date, the window thrown
open at her birth to let the world in, and slid shut
to keep her body warm a little longer.

Kneeling, I pull a milk-eyed Mason jar
of vodka tonic, which she loved as much
as I hate, and a shortbread from my pocket.
I peel the tangerine into thready petals attached
at the stem, into the white-veined rays
of a star, into a stilled canvas,

Vanishing Man with Liquor, Citrus, Grave and Cookie,

and I eat, I drink,
every bitter crumb and drop,
for all the lives I've lost.

A part offered at the hooves of the bay and paint down the street from where we lived once, along with a bag of carrots and apples. Samuel had no concept of a life as huge as a horse, what its muscled bucks and leaps might mean. He waved to a one-eyed mare champing the hollow rod of a carrot, her head and socket shaped by a teenager with a nailed-through two-by-four. If not for the shock wire strung over the fence, I would have let him touch her face.

Ezra, my son, my mortal boy, please, please forgive me.

Five years ago, I did not die with you, and I will not die now without you.

> Sleepless again, I
> lay my hand on the smooth branches
> of his ribs, the soft
> pebbles of his spine, his breath
> a stream untorn by my touch.

—Horse Run, October 20th

Dropped Tanka

His grandfather walked
off a roof. His brother walked
out of a fig tree.
I flung my grief-worn limbs into
the green eyes of cenotes,

to forget myself
for a second, until panic
stabbed through. He leapt away
from me when I had lifted him
high enough to touch the tip

of a hanging signboard,
just past the carts, as always.
His mother, paper-
dolled by sunlight, called out, slipping
between the glass doors. Mid laugh,

his heels dug, and he
kicked into bare air. We all
held our long smiles, waited
for a flash, for an echo,
for a quick caught belt loop,

waited for a kind gust
of wind, for gravity to
forgive him my weak
arms, until his head clapped the tile
like wood, born to be broken.

*   *   *

We all learn one day:
something dropped is something lost.
Out of reach means *gone*

forever, bits of childhood locked
in a mirror of pond water.

He watched my mouth, *Lost,*
lost, thrusted against the railing
reaching for the spot,
the splash where his toy had been
thrown, then dove, and disappeared.

Once below, all sound
stopped. The plastic tiger sunk,
watching a boy cry
by skyfuls its wavering life,
its eternal inch of silt.

A part, a silent heap laid on the iron and concrete foot of a trestle of the rail-bridge that passes over the cove, left for someone else to find, or the wind to carry off, bury at sea.

We woke to crows arguing over a loaf of bread forgotten under a table. Dawn greyed its way out of the waves. We left Jenny to sleep off a long night of hard ground and relentless nursing. Samuel ran ahead to join the jawing birds, the cackle of wings, and whimper when they scattered.

I shadowed him from the parking lot to the bluffs to the tar-scarred low tide. Squirrels thumped into the landslid cliffs to get away from us. He curled my fingers around each whittled clamshell he found, each copper bulb of seaweed, every unfamiliar thing his eye could gather.

Birds leapt ahead of us, back toward the bridge, its hundred foot beams rusting in air. We stopped at the foundation of a trestle and arranged each object into a line, a point of light in your name. I tipped out the bottle, blot of white on orange. A train came and rattled our constellation apart, made the trestles hum, made the wind blow.

> We gather breakage,
> shells, wood to build words. Animals
> thud in the damp bank,
> startled by my footfalls, a weak voice
> calling out, *Daddy, come back.*

—Gaviota

Easter Morning

I try to tell myself this place belongs
to everyone, not just the quiet families
looking to make church in dry riverbeds
and groves of thirst-split oaks,
not just a pair of greying hippies flopped
on a white boulder, or a son on shoulders
driving his father-shaped horse by the hair,
or his mother silently slipping ahead
to hide plastic eggs by the trailside.

But, Christ, somebody's radio back
at the trailhead keeps getting louder
the farther we walk up the valley wall,
a Spanish station cranked high enough
to muffle the grump of an old generator,
trumpet lines and guitar licks slapping
every stone, acorn, threadbare blackberry,
child and hiker for miles around.
Roasted peanuts and blackened corn husks,
the bitterer smells of a large gathering,
a reunion maybe, echo off the tree trunks.

We came here to be alone, or feel alone
at least, surrounded by what God made,
but now there's music everywhere, warbling
choruses I can't quite catch, meditate away
or stop myself from resenting, from looking
back at each treebreak for a quick glimpse
of whoever thought to bring a PA system
to the National Forest on a Sunday morning.

Turning a bend, Samuel tugs my chin
toward a blue egg Jenny stashed
in the withering shade under a fern.
'Nuther blue one, he calls. She grins,

pretending to be amazed that he could spot
such a well-hidden jewel. I toddle down,
suddenly aware of how much heavier
he's become lately, and hand Sam the egg.
In one bell-half of the plastic shell he finds
a lozenge of clear, smooth quartz, in the other
a pine cone the size of a pinky nail.
He holds them both in front of my eyes,
squealing, until I stumble on a root and realize
the radio cut out some moments ago.

Like nothing, Samuel drops the stone
and crumbles the pine cone between
his thumb and finger. *Again, again,*
he says, his voice still babyish, asking only
to find whatever's precious in this place,
not to carry or keep it as his own.

I hear girls laughing back by the river, clanging
pots and bottles, guttering through the wash,
singing. *Otra vez, otra vez,* maybe.

A part for the burled, burnt out heart of a thousand year old tree. I'd thought to sow you into the roots of a sapling redwood, to make you its first taste of ash with so many seasons of wildfire to come. Instead, I pressed you into the lip of a scar, hole become body, gave you a thumb's width of 243 lightning-carved feet of flesh.

Down the trail, I could hear Jenny cry out, her arm stretched to catch Samuel's collar, his arm stretched to feed the arrowhead of a leaf to a squirrel on a fencepost, becoming more his brother every day.

> Where this light comes from,
> these starved clouds yawning after
> one bird in a fist
> of branches— where this sudden courage
> comes from, I will not question.

—Henry Cowell Redwoods

Undated Photograph (Beach)

A wide, blank beach behind him:
he stares at his hand, his forefinger
split, pointing away slightly, as if
to dip into the wind, as if a thought
had just now whistled through him,
cracking one door, latching another.

The first thing: take
all the string in the world.

Tie his fingertip to the far-off flintspark
of a gull drafting. Tie the gull's bright beak
to the splash in a bucket at surfline.
Tie an angry fish to the guttural roll
of pebbles against an abuelo's boot,
feet to footsteps washed smooth, footsteps
to fishhooks. Tie the old man's beard
to the pier-posts to the waves
to the boats to the earth curving away
and carrying us all through space
while the sun stays still where it stays, tied
finally back to the tip of his wistful finger.

Now: reach out and rattle
the thread, by hand or breath.

The world trembles on.
He squints. A gull gusts up
and down like burnt paper.
A fish sloughs against the walls
of its bucket, churning a fat bloom
of scales to hide in. A fisherman
toes for crabs beneath the pebbles
and tugs his aching beard to a point,
his eyes stuck somewhere

beyond the horizon.
Your son turns to you, seeming
to forget whatever he saw in himself.
He cups out a handful of warm sand,
tosses it at your knees. He waves
you closer. Grinning above him,
he tries to climb the tower
of your legs and body, as if
he were a little boy still,
and well. Out of breath,
he grabs your neck, draws
your face to his, flushed hands
weighted on your shoulders,
and kisses you on the lips
while the boats drift
and the ocean falters,
while the earth falls forward
and the sun keeps still.

Then: into your ear,
he says, *listen.*
Listen.

A part, a year: a calf lowed in the next paddock, ambling toward us to sniff our fists for ragweed or dandelion leaves. Samuel, hip-tall, and I scraped away soft red dust to fill with soft white ashes. With only a few seconds of his attention, I cradled his face so he'd know to repeat my words. *"I…"*

"I."

"Love…"

"Love."

"You…"

"You."

But before I could get him to say *"Ezra"*, he blurted out "Daddy!", clapping, because that's how we've practiced those words. Because right now he can only name what he can see, and touch.

At the fence, the calf rutted her head on a post, pushed closer. Nose crossed by woven wire, her warm, wet breath drifted heavy into our hands. Samuel loved her completely.

> How do I describe
> two sons that can never touch,
> wrestle, race, laugh as one,
> when what I must say is this:
>
> All ties go to the living.

—Roberts Ranch, Behind the Preschool, October 20th

Bread

Ezra swings hard until his body angles into the earth, his legs
and hips almost too much for the chain and rubber sling.
He swings until the bar rattles its apex, the jolt after
a sudden second of weightlessness, until all
I can see of him is a curve with a face, a grinning ray
       about to shoot off through the sky.

       *

The small Pakistani boy fishhooks my eye, hunched
over on a bench at a playground. There is a circle
of children behind him, waiting stars on an arabesque.
Do you have any bread? he asks breathlessly, my face
domed in the telescopes of his glasses.

Nope, I tell him, because it's the truth.

Pretend, he says with a whip of his wrists as if tossing a doll.
He huffs and flicks his hands again. The doll becomes a juggler's pin.
Pretend you have bread, man, he whines and casts back
his head, the pin become something much greater,
and more necessary.

So I reach into my pocket and pull out air,
cupping it in front of our faces. The children's eyes tick
with our movements. He reaches into the warm
concave of my hands to pull out air.
Pinching it in front of him, he returns to the circle
and fists out loaves to his starving friends.
Soon enough, they're back for more,
for soda, spaghetti, cheeseburgers, sun-
soft bowls of ice cream.
       I give them all I have.

*

Ezra swings higher and harder now, nearly gone. There, for a flicker—
his eyewhites, the quick meniscus of a smile, and then
he is nothing but a pendulum blade,
    a threaded spider in a doorway, a stone about to fly,
        the centuries-long ellipsis of a comet.

A Note on Forms

Haibun is the Japanese name for 17th Century poet-monk Basho Matsuo's poetic-prose travel journals, which are buttressed by haiku. Contemporary haibun is a combination of prose and poetry, either haiku or tanka, sometimes described as 'a narrative of epiphany' (Contemporary Haibun Online).

Many writers of haiku or tanka in English forgo the historical Japanese syllabification of the forms, 5-7-5 and 5-7-5-7-7 respectively, in order to focus on aspects that are considered more essential: imagism, shortened syntax, a sense of 'being there' and a poetic turn in the leap between images. I came to these forms, however, as a way of beginning to write again after the long poetic silence of my grief. As such, I found the limiting structure of the syllable count to be a comfort, in that I knew the poem, often still painful to write, must end within those bounds. A hard count also requires great discipline, a dedication to saying as much as I can as elegantly and memorably as I can in that small moment of the reader's attention. The voice that I have found in these forms is not meant to be emblematic of the current, rich conversation with tradition taking place among many writers of contemporary haiku, but as what brought me back to poetry in a dire time, which is enough for me to stand by it.

Notes on Places

"—Toward Tulum, November": facing the Caribbean Sea on 40-foot cliffs, the walled Mayan city of Tulum was a major port for the city of Cobá on the eastern coast of the Yucatán Peninsula. Tulum, a colonial name, means *wall*. A thurible is a metal censer suspended from chains, in which incense is burned for religious ceremonies.

"—Nohoch Mul": meaning *large hill,* the Nohoch Mul pyramid is the center of the Mayan city of Cobá, which means *waters stirred by a wind.* At 137 feet, it is the tallest pyramid in the Yucatán.

"—Big Sur": sur means *south.* A yurt is a round, semi-permanent tent, popular as lodging on the Big Sur coast of Central California.

"—Pascagoula": Pascagoula, Mississippi, takes its name from the extinct Pascagoula tribe of Native Americans, *bread eaters,* who are said to have drowned themselves in the river that shares their name rather than be enslaved by the neighboring Biloxi tribe.

"—Forest Falls": with an over-500 foot cumulative drop, Big Falls in Forest Falls, California, is the largest year-round waterfall in Southern California.

"—Coronado": Spanish for *crowned one,* Coronado is a tied island off the coast of San Diego, California. The beach is warm and soft. Navy Seals train there.

"—Riverside": named for the Santa Ana River, Riverside, California, is the most populous city in the Inland Empire and the birthplace of the California citrus industry.

"—Kitchen Counter": A friend of mine worked at the County Coroner's office at time of Ezra's death, so she was able to prepare Ezra for cremation and to place his ashes into two large glass boxes and two small glass vials for his mother and me. She was the last person to see his body, to sing to him and kiss his head, and to push the final button that sent his body into the fire. I wanted to do it, but I let her talk me out of it.

"—Liquidambar": the liquidamabar, or Sweetgum family, named for the sweetness of their sap when cut, are deciduous trees known for their hardiness and bold display of autumnal colors. As bonsai, they're decent beginning trees, able to withstand over and underwatering better than most.

"—Pomegranate Tree, June": living between two orange groves, a mile from California Citrus State Park, Ezra and I became used to sounds and smells not found elsewhere in Riverside. There is the scent of blossoms when the wind changes, the chug of frost propellers running through the night, coyotes and roosters heckling each other. I love the home I've made with Jenny, but some part of me will always long for the home I had with Ezra and Sylvia.

"—Na'Pali": Hawaiian for *high cliffs*, so named for the 4,000 green cliffs rising from the ocean, the Na'Pali Coast of Kauai is best seen by boat, with spinner dolphins leaping alongside.

"—Secret Falls": Secret Falls is the common name for Uluwehi Falls, for its *lush, flourishing plants*, in the Wailua River basin on Kauai.

"—Nu'uanu Pali": the Pali lookout, with its howling wind, is the site of the decisive Battle of Nu'uanu in 1795, in which King Kamehameha I united Oahu by driving hundreds of his enemies over the 1,000 foot cliff to the valley below.

"—Byodo-In Temple": the Hawaiian Byodo-In Temple in the Valley of the Temples, commissioned in 1968 to celebrate the centennial of the introduction of Japanese culture to the islands, is a scale replica of the original Byodo-In Temple founded in 1052 near the ancient city of Kyoto.

"—Manoa": meaning *thick, thickness, deep* or *depth*, the trail to Manoa Falls on Oahu has stood for lush jungle in numerous films, including *Jurassic Park* and *Raiders of the Lost Ark*.

"—Keyhole": the Keyhole reef formation at Hanauma Bay on Oahu. According to the park ranger who took my report, the nature preserve is sometimes called "Heartbreak Bay" because of all the wedding bands lost there. To wit, the ranger kept a ring mandrel and sizer in her desk to aid in filing lost ring reports.

"—Library, July 20th": I became an elementary librarian after a few years of odd jobs after Ezra died. I love it, underappreciated as librarians can be, and there are times when I think this might be exactly where all the reading out loud I've done, to Ezra, to Sylvia, at festivals and open mics, was leading me.

"—Hillside": Beside crows, I see hummingbirds near my home more than any other bird. It never occurred to me that when I see a hummingbird, or the cat brings me one, it is most likely in transit, somewhere between Canada and Costa Rica.

"—Reveille": French for *wake up*, reveille is a bugle tune traditionally played at sunrise on military installations such as the air force base near my home.

"—Los Angeles": the Los Angeles Times Festival of Books is the largest book festival in the United States, held every April on the University of Southern California campus.

"—Ultrasound": sometimes I am drawn to spread ashes because the moment, rather than the place, inspires it. Then I have to search for the beauty in the spot to match the moment, like a blanketing of dress-shaped jacaranda blossoms on a hill of new grass in the grey center of a hospital parking lot.

"—North Ponto": North Ponto is a tiny access point to South Carlsbad State Beach in Carlsbad, California, with soft sand and heel-battering rocks just inside the surfline. Ponto is Portuguese for *point* or *speck*, which might just be a coincidence.

"—Fig Grove, July 20th": covering 40 acres in the foothills of the Box Spring Mountains, the Botanic Gardens at UC Riverside are one of the abiding landmarks of my adult life. Ezra and I bouldered, played tag, climbed trees there. Jenny and I built our family there.

"—Labor & Delivery": as with Ezra, I had what felt like a private moment with Samuel immediately after he was born and was getting cleaned, wrapped and beanied under the warming lights. His eyes seemed to lock on mine, and his crying broke for the first time in his life. As with Ezra, I am honored to have been the first solid, unmoving object for him to find in this blinding world.

"—North Ponto and a Year": there is a heavy, black sand, maybe garnet or tourmaline, that runs under the lighter, quartzoze sand at North Ponto. When a wave runs over something written in the sand, the black minerals hold the shape of the word two or three waves before smudging to nothing.

"—Children's Hospital": I am ever grateful that Ezra was able to be treated at Loma Linda University Medical Center, which features one of the first broadly applied Proton Radiation Therapy programs in the country. When Ezra needed to get out of the hospital bed and get his blood moving, we would often walk down to the lobby to watch the blinking light race around a simple model of the subterranean particle accelerator beneath us.

"—Evergreen Memorial Park & Mausoleum": established in 1872, many renowned Riverside residents are buried in the historic section of Evergreen Cemetery, including John W. North, founder of Riverside, and Eliza Tibbets, who planted the first navel orange in California.

"—Horse Run, October 20th": Ezra and I shot several mock wildlife documentaries in Sylvia's backyard and the surrounding groves using his plush handpuppets as predator and prey. In our short film *Foodchain*, we used the sound of the horses down the street crunching carrots and soft apples as the soundtrack for one puppet devouring another.

"—Gaviota": meaning *seagull*, Gaviota Beach, north of Santa Barbara, California, is famous for its harsh wind, tarstreaked waves and an enormous rail bridge.

"—Henry Cowell Redwoods": the tallest tree in Henry Cowell Redwoods State Park, northeast of Santa Cruz, California, stands 277 feet tall and is 1,500 years old.

"—Roberts Ranch, Behind the Preschool, October 20th": since writing this poem, the owners of Roberts Ranch have raised an additional fence keeping the public from their cows, horses and single mule. I suppose this is in answer to parents from the preschool stopping daily to pet, or feed, the livestock, which is perfectly understandable.

Acknowledgements

I thank the editors of the following publications and anthologies in which these poems, some in different versions, first appeared or are forthcoming.

BODY: "Custer's Last Haircut", "Snabu"; *Sixfold*: "Folk Medicine" (formerly "Medicine"), "First Dream of Kinship" (formerly "Kin"), "Dropped Tanka", "A Love Poem"; *Tupelo Quarterly*: "South Wichita Safeway"; *Ruminate*: "Condolences"; *The Turnip Truck(s)*: "A Story I Remembered…"; *The Wild Lemon Project:* "Undated Photograph (Beach)" *LETTERS*: "Negligent Avocadicide"; *Slice Magazine:* "Armadillo", "Notes from the Life After" (formerly "Notes From Another Life"); *Tin Cannon:* "Love to All, S~" (formerly "As Always, Love To All, Sylvia"), "Flagstaff", "First Dream In Which The Wind…"; *Kindred Magazine:* "Hunting Accident", "Undated Photograph (PICU)," "Metaphor Game", "First, Language" (formerly "Sur Means South"); *The Coachella Review:* "Self-Hypnosis"; *The Atticus Review:* "Bread".

"I Can Take It" was published in *The Cancer Poetry Project 2*, edited by Karin B. Miller, published by Tasora Books, 2013.

"Now, Someday" was published in *Best New Poets 2013*, edited by Guest Editor Brenda Shaughnessy and Series Editor Jazzy Danziger, published by The University of Virginia Press, 2013.

"Grandpa", "Now, Someday (reprint)", and "I Can Take It (reprint)" were published in *The Burden of Light: Poems on Illness and Loss*, edited by Tanya Chernov, published by Foreword Literary, 2014.

All writings attributed to Ezra Phoenix Chatterton, including the haiku that appear in "—Riverside", the letter appearing on page 19 and the text messages appearing on pages 32, 39, and 43, are that author's unique creations, held in copyright by his estate.

Micah Chatterton writes, edits, teaches and tends library at various locations in the Inland Empire, where he grew up. His work has appeared in a number of journals, including *B O D Y*, *Sixfold*, *Ruminate*, *Tupelo Quarterly*, *LETTERS*, and *Slice*. His work is also featured in *Best New Poets 2013* (University of Virginia Press, 2013), *The Cancer Poetry Project 2* (Thasora Books, 2013) and *The Burden of Light: Poems on Illness and Loss* (Foreword Literary, 2014).

www.ingramcontent.com/pod-product-compliance
Lightning Source LLC
Chambersburg PA
CBHW020940090426
42736CB00010B/1209